I0841048

THE CEO AUTHOR

The Business Owner's Guide to Expanding
Your Thought Leadership with a Book

PORSCHÉ MYSTICQUE STEELE

Acknowledgments

Thank you to my soulmate, my Handsome, my Saint James. Without you, nothing would be possible. This all exists because of you. Thank you, my King. I love you.

Thank you to my #1 cheerleader, my momma, and the squad who always had my back; Akiya, Fehed, Akasha, and Masao. I love you.

Thank you to Elaine Powell for guiding me into my Thought Leadership. My life, my business, and my potential have truly expanded because of you. Thank you.

Thank you to Tamara Rasheed for transforming me into a selfless author and helping me cultivate my integrity. Your love, energy, and dedication to my growth will continue to blow my mind. Thank you.

Big thank you to my MysticqueRose Publishing team; Maria, Esther, Kristina, Milos, and Seun. You all will always have a special place in my heart. Your hard work, dedication, and loyalty will never cease to amaze me. Thank you so, so much.

Contents

Introduction

Many business owners strive for the same goal: to expand their business, impact as many lives as possible, and deepen their influence while doing it.

Unfortunately, this seems to be the main source of struggle for many of us. Relying mainly on maintaining a social media presence and networking, many business leaders fail to be seen as the go-to expert and be recognized across the globe.

Is this you?

Have you been frustrated by the number of verified experts who are getting Netflix specials while you're merely being viewed on YouTube and Instagram?

Does it stress you to see massive summits and panels that feature your peers as keynote speakers and special guests, yet, you had to buy a ticket to attend?

What if I told you that the issue wasn't phantom gatekeeping at Netflix? The problem isn't your level of expertise being compared to your peers, and it most certainly isn't the organizers and directors who fail to recognize your credibility.

The problem is YOU.

As you move through this book, you will be birthing the author within you. In doing so, it will change who you are, how you move in life, and how you show up. This change will cause people to look at you differently. Your energy will be different. In a room full of people, you will stand out.

This book is the first step of your evolution into true Thought Leadership.

By the time you finish reading, your transformation will be well underway. I guarantee that who you are now and who you will become by the end of this, will not be the same person.

No longer will you be playing small.

You will no longer waste time and money going to networking events and still be unseen and unrecognized among the major execs.

You will no longer participate in collaboration books hoping that your one chapter will be enough to boost your credibility and visibility.

With this book, you will be able to create a book of your own that launches you directly into the room with the elites.

With your book, you will immediately be positioned as the go-to expert in your industry. Your name will be listed among the globally influential CEOs and founders.

The possibilities are NOT endless; they are intentional and specific.

With your book, we will create those possibilities and live inside of them.

Everything will change.

You must prepare.

Before you move forward, I would like to note that the way I've written this book is quite different from the way I deliver talks or coach authors one-on-one. You'll read in chapter one how your identity determines the relationship you have with your readers. I want you to understand that for the sake of this book, our relationship must be that of teacher/student.

I typically dislike this relationship when I coach. I found that a friend/friend relationship works much better when attempting to help someone transform their life. So, if you're reading this and you know a bit about my character and how bubbly and friendly

I am, I must apologize; that is not what you will get from this book.

In order to truly serve you and help you achieve the results you're looking for; I must step into the role of an educator. I must guide you using hard facts and painful truths. Once you've completed this book, however, I ask that you reach out to me so that you and I may transform our relationship into one that is most befitting (and much more fun) to get you to the next level.

This journey won't be easy, but if you are prepared to fully and completely transform, I guarantee you will get the results you are hoping for.

I recommend you keep a notepad and writing tool nearby so you may jot down everything that comes up for you as you read.

Congratulations in advance for what you are about to accomplish and who you are about to become!

Sincerely,

~Porsché Mysticque Steele

PART

I

BIRTHING THE AUTHOR WITHIN

CHAPTER I

Who Are You?

Business owners who have made a deep impact on their communities can answer this question with ease. Those leaders understand who they are, what they're worth, and what they want to be remembered for. These three things allow them to show up with confidence in any place, at any time, and most especially, in a book.

The great thing about confidence is that it is felt, not heard.

This is what sets people like Tony Robbins, Steve Jobs, and Oprah Winfrey apart from the rest of the world. They never have to say who they are, what they're worth, or what they want to be remembered for. As their audience, we already know simply by watching them enter a room or step on a stage.

Can you say the same thing?

Who are you?

What is your worth?

What do you want to be remembered for?

The answer to these three questions will determine the type of author that you will be and the impact your book will have. If you fail to answer them for yourself, you will be like every other person who impulsively releases a book, continuing to be generally unknown and unrecognized, failing to make an impact, and leaving behind an underwhelming legacy.

They haven't taken the time to think about their identity, their value, or their legacy. They simply felt like they had a story to tell, and they dove head-first, with reckless abandon, into telling it without any regard for what the book was meant to do for them or their reader.

This is a mistake.

#1 - Who Are You?

Don't tell me your name. Don't tell me what you do for a living. Tell me who you are.

How would you describe yourself? Or better yet, how would your family and friends describe you?

Are you bright, bubbly, and energetic? Or are you serious, straightforward, and stern?

Whoever you are and however people describe you, this is who you will be to your readers.

It is this description that will ultimately dictate the type of relationship you have with your audience. Will it be a teacher/student relationship? Friend/Friend? Lecturer/Listener?

Before you put pen to paper, ask yourself, who do you want to be for your readers? How do you want them to see you? Take a moment to reflect on this and decide.

Be aware that who you are is simply a decision that you get to make. The description you were given about yourself is only true if you decide it is. You have the power to make those characteristics true or false.

So, if you want to be fun, informative, and inspiring to your readers, then be that person starting now. Begin to live your everyday life being fun, informative, and inspiring. The choice is yours and what you choose is what your readers will get.

#2 - What Is Your Worth?

How valuable are you? How expensive is your knowledge? Your time? Your energy? People often find it strange to attach a value to themselves. Some even find it egotistical or vain. I wholeheartedly disagree. Knowing what you are worth is both beautiful and powerful.

I hold my peace, my time, and my affection close to my chest, and I am very selective about who I give it to. I spent my teen and early adult years giving this away for free, and every time I did, it was immediately taken for granted. People simply stopped caring about whether or not I had the emotional bandwidth to handle a situation or deal with their issues. They stopped asking me, "Porsché, are you free to help me with an issue?" and instead would say, "Porsché, call me. I need help with an issue." Since I didn't know my worth, I would make the call, no questions asked. My cup was always empty.

Eventually, I said enough was enough, and I began to attach a price to every aspect of my life. Yet, the more I began to recognize my worth, the more I realized that the value I offered to those who could afford it, did not match. I was unfairly expensive! So, I began to increase my value. The price of my time, knowledge, and affection didn't change, but the value of it did.

As an author, when the value of what you offer matches the price you set for it, you create an everlasting bond between you and your readers. Readers will understand that you come at a steep price, and to be able to enroll themselves into your universe would be a blessing. Most importantly, they will know that once they step inside, their lives will be changed forever. The value of what they get matches the price they paid for it.

In order for the above to be true for you, you must establish your worth and your value first.

So, I ask again, what is your worth?

#3 - What Do You Want to Be Remembered For?

Too often do authors write books without thinking about future impact. They're mostly concerned with how the book will fair on the market. How many copies will I sell? How many people will read it? How many people will leave a review?

These questions only satisfy an immediate curiosity. But what about 20 years from now? Books never go out of style, so your story has the potential to be around for generations. It is imperative that you take the time to produce something that you can be proud of decades from now.

Your book will still be around even after you die and people will still read your story after you've been gone for ages. What do you want them to say? What do you want them to think?

Any book that you produce becomes a part of your legacy. So, what will that legacy be?

What is it that you want to be remembered for?

In truth, it isn't easy to answer these questions. Sometimes we find it easier to just write what's in our hearts. Who wants to take the time to work out all this mindset stuff before penning?

I understand the objection, but I also recognize that this is the main reason why many authors fail. You are meant to be an above-average business leader; thus, you must be an above-average author. But being a good author isn't just about how verbose you are or how well you can put a sentence together. Being an incredible author boils down to the experience you deliver to your readers.

I invite you to leave your objections at the door. They'll bring you nothing but failure.

Before moving on to the next chapter, take time to reflect and journal about those questions and get clear on the author you want to become.

Takeaway: Before you can write a book, you have to know who you are (your identity), what you're worth (the value you offer), and what you want to be remembered for (your legacy). Only then will you know the best way to serve your readers.

CHAPTER 2

The Author's Promise

It's a sad truth that authors today lack integrity. Understand this: The moment you publish a book, you make a promise to your reader. Every book that has ever been written contains a promise; the promise to be entertained, the promise to be inspired, or the promise to be educated.

Readers are aware of this promise too. The reader/author relationship is undoubtedly a selfish one on the part of the reader. The author gives and the reader takes. That's how it's always been and that is how it will remain.

When we as readers pick up a book, the first thing we think to ourselves is, "What will I get out of this? What's in it for me?" Rarely does a reader read a book for the sake of the author. That is unless the reader is a close relative or friend of the author; and if the author is writing solely for friends and relatives, then they are doomed from the start.

Nevertheless, readers have every right to be selfish. They must be! The more selfish the reader is, the more beneficial it is to the author.

If you feed your readers with a sweet, delicious, and nutritious meal that makes them feel energized and excited, I guarantee they will come back for more.

But if you're serving up slop with no taste and no nutritional value, they will run for the hills, and you'll be left with nothing.

Unfortunately, this is no longer common knowledge. The ease of independent publishing has given millions the opportunity to publish empty books filled with unhealthy slop. They rush to force this "meal" in front of the face of readers, hoping that they'll take just a small bite. Some readers may, and they'll leave the table with a bad taste in their mouths. Others can smell the rancid silage before they even see what's on the plate.

You must ask yourself, what kind of author do I want to be?

Do you want to feed your readers gunk or do you want to offer them sustenance and nutriment?

It isn't enough to simply recognize your promise as an author, you must also actively deliver on it with every word you write. Every drip of your ink should be saturated with your kept promise.

In order to successfully keep your promise to your readers, you have to have integrity as an author. To have integrity as an author, you must also have integrity as a human being and practice it in your daily life. Many people don't realize that they've lacked integrity from the start.

I invite you to complete the following exercise to test your integrity.

Simply answer yes or no to the following questions and record your answer.

1. In the past month, have you been more than 10 minutes late to an appointment?

2. In the past month, have you forgotten to show up at an appointment?

3. In the past month, have you told someone that you would do something by a certain day or time and failed to do so on that EXACT date or that EXACT time?

4. If you failed to do these things, did you also fail to genuinely apologize, own the failure, and recommit?

5. In the past month, have you intentionally lied about something or falsified circumstances?

If you answered yes to three or more of these questions, then you lack integrity. Integrity is more than not lying. It's also being a person of your word. If you say you'll do something, you do it exactly as you stated.

For example, if you told your mom that you would call her that evening, you don't wait until the next evening to call, you don't call in the afternoon or the next morning. You call her **that** evening.

If you told your client you would send over a document at 3 pm, don't send it at 2 pm or 5 pm; send it at 3 because you said you would.

Integrity is also holding yourself accountable. Things often happen and get in our way to cause distraction or deviation from our plans. Instead of blaming the distraction, integrity will allow you to recognize your role in the deviation. When mistakes are made or we fail to be our word, we must not only recognize the failure for ourselves but it must be stated plainly to all those involved. That is true accountability.

Being realistic is another way to have integrity. Many of us are eager to jump in and help others or be a part of something amazing. But in those moments of excitement, we tend to overcommit. It's better to be realistic about what you can and cannot do so you don't place yourself in a position in which you are unable to keep promises you've made.

Starting today, I want you to practice integrity. If you practice integrity every day, by the time you're ready to start writing your book, you'll easily write with the reader in mind. You'll find yourself instinctively looking for more ways to add value to your book. Or perhaps you'll find yourself doing more research to ensure the information you are giving is accurate.

Having integrity as an author is a powerful asset that will undoubtedly set you apart from the rest.

Takeaway: Integrity is what great authors use to deliver on their promise to their readers. Begin to practice integrity every day to strengthen your ability to uphold the author's promise.

CHAPTER 3

Your Legacy

In Chapter 1, you got clear on what it is you want to be remembered for. This is perhaps the most powerful question you can ask yourself as you begin to birth your book. It is the moment in which you determine your legacy and the foundation of your impact and global change.

You must understand that this is what you have the potential to create; global change.

Any book that does not support your legacy is a wasted book not worth publishing. We currently find ourselves in an age where too many books are created, thrown into the wild for general consumption, and have zero impact on the world.

This practice has tainted the once-beautiful process of self-publishing, but you will not be a part of that frenzy. You will move forward with a book of intention, a book that is proudly a permanent part of your legacy.

Let's begin by defining "legacy."

According to Oxford Languages, legacy is "the long-lasting impact of particular events, actions, etc. that took place in the past, or of a person's life."

Based on this definition, your book would serve as one of the longest-lasting sources of impact from your life.

Take a moment to process this and understand the weight that your book will carry. Everything you put on your pages will be your memorial.

But remember, your legacy and your book are NOT for you. It's for those who will need it once you're gone. You are not writing this book for you; you're writing it for them.

So, what is it that you want to leave for them? What do you want them to have when you're no longer around to give it to them personally?

This is something I originally struggled with.

For years, I couldn't see past my own desire. My ego was what drove me to become a speaker. It fueled my desire to be a globally recognized coach. But this fuel was tainted. The more I chased my own satisfaction, the further I ran away from my ability to be a great coach, author, and human being.

When authors make this mistake, we fall into a trap called "selfish publishing."

Selfish publishing is the act of writing and releasing a book simply to satisfy your own ego. In selfish publishing, the author has no regard for the reader and is disinterested in the reader's satisfaction or transformation.

Over the years, I have come across many individuals who were on the path of selfish publishing. I do not fault them nor do I pass judgment. It has been ingrained in our brains to desire to write a book simply because we've led movie-worthy lives. We look at what we've been through and think, "I have an incredible story and should tell it." But have you ever asked yourself why?

When I pose this question to those individuals, I typically hear the same type of answers:

"I've been through a lot and I think people should hear it."

"People keep telling me I should write a book about my life."

I then tell them to dig deeper. Why should people hear it? Why should you put it in a book?

It normally takes several minutes to find that why, but the more you dig, the less selfish your intention becomes. Soon, you'll settle on what you want your readers to get from your story.

This outcome will be part of your legacy. What your readers will get when they've finished reading your book will be what you're remembered for.

Allow me to give you a bit of perspective:

Imagine for a moment that you are a ghost. You've been gone for years, and now you're watching over members of your family who purchased a copy of your book. What effect does it have on them? Do they cherish it? Or has it been sitting on their shelves untouched for years?

What about those you don't know? Are they referring back to your book to help solve a new issue in their lives? Are they sharing it with their family and friends because they got exactly what they were looking for?

These reactions should constantly be at the forefront of your mind and nothing else because this will be your legacy. Not the number of reviews, not the number of books sold, and not the number of likes and comments.

Focus on the true reaction of your reader and what you will leave them with. When you do, you will find that your book will effortlessly make a massive impact and forever change the way people describe you.

Takeaway: The impact your book has on your readers will be a part of your legacy, good or bad. Decide what you want that to be.

PART

II

BUILDING THE BOOK

CHAPTER 4

What's Your Story?

One of the greatest assets every business owner has is their story. No matter what you do or the niche you're in, your story will always be your strongest advantage.

What makes you an expert is the journey that you've gone through and the things you learned along the way. Unfortunately, as CEOs, only a fraction of our stories get told. Sure, we have to share some of our experiences so that we're relatable and are able to create deeper connections with the people we serve. Sure, that single line from your story is impactful and eye-opening. But imagine the level of transformation you could make if your entire story were told!

Don't just take my word for it. How many times have you shared a part of your journey? Whether it was to a potential client, as a part of your brand story, on a stage, or on your social media channels. Now, out of those, how many times did someone respond with, "You should write a book!" or ask, "Do you have a book out?"

Happens often, doesn't it? This is proof that even a fraction of your story has created enough impact to make people yearn for more, and you have the ability to give it to them.

The question is, what is your most impactful story?

In reality, our lives are not one long sequence. It is a compilation of many different moments (or stories) that we've lived through over the years. So, which of these stories caused your biggest transformation? Which ones shaped and molded you into who you are now?

Hold that story in your mind. Try to remember where you were, who you were with, and how old you were. Imagine the finer details of that story and hold it. This story and everything surrounding it is what will change the lives of your readers. Your story gives them the chance to experience the sometimes traumatic and tragic events that could lead to their transformation without having to go through it themselves. That is a gift that is truly priceless.

Though I had multiple stories to tell, there was one in particular that gave me my biggest transformation and has the most impact on the people I share it with.

THE STORY

My biggest transformation occurred about two years into my marriage. By that point, I had already left the toxic environment I was living in back in America and had moved to Nigeria. My husband was working hard in medical school and I was progressing in my business. We were both happy in our marriage. Yet, the one thing that kept darkening my rosy life was the nightmares.

Every night, I would dream about the physical and sexual abuse that had happened back home. I would dream about my escape, but instead of successfully making it out as I had in real life, I was always caught, dragged back, and shot, beaten, or worse. The constant nightmares began to take a toll on my mental and emotional health. I was constantly tired and I was losing the ability to enjoy the things that used to make me happy. I knew I couldn't go on like that. So, I began to focus on my personal development. I hired several coaches, enrolled in various programs, and worked my ass off.

It was one program in particular, Landmark Worldwide, that helped me realize that all the work I had put in was only a fraction of what I needed to do in order to heal myself. I had to own what I went through and accept the abuse for what it was instead of attempting to bury it. In order to embrace what happened, I had to do two things: 1) Confront the person who was responsible, and 2) Share and speak about my story.

Even though I knew this was what I had to do, I refused. I gave myself one excuse after the other.

"It's too late where he is. I'll call later."

"I know he won't answer."

"No one wants to hear my story."

"They'll think that I am weak."

My brain was full of objections. Finally, I decided to suck it up and call him. I hadn't spoken to him since I left two years prior. With sweaty palms and a lump in my throat, I dialed his number.

Ring.... ring.... ring...

Finally, the ringing stopped and I heard his voice, "Hello, you've reached…" It was his voicemail.

Though I don't fully remember what I said, I remember that as I spoke after the beep, my voice was shaky. Try as I might, I couldn't steady my vocal cords.

Not even ten minutes after I left the voicemail, he texted me saying that he was available to chat. I inhaled sharply as I stared at his message.

Why was I so scared?

I knew how hurt he was by me leaving the way I did, but for 10 years, I was subjected to his abuse. From age 16 to 26, I lived with that pain, and truly, he did a damn good job of making me forget the hurt and accept what was happening as a good thing.

But I was an adult now and at some point, you have to realize that some things are not and never have been "okay." I refused to feel an ounce of remorse or guilt for taking control of my life.

I pressed the call icon and listened to the short three rings before he answered. His greeting was low and calm, as if he'd been expecting a call from me since the day I left. No excitement, no nervousness. Steady and neutral.

Just the mojo I needed to get myself right.

We exchanged minor pleasantries, "How are you?" "How are things?" but I cut it short. Without a single pause, I told him, "I wanted to talk to you about some things."

I explained the personal development I had been making and how I had evolved. I told him that I made a commitment to myself to fully embrace my authenticity and not just for me but for everyone and everything. As I live inside of my authenticity, I'm no longer holding on to the secrecy, the unspoken truths, and the lies. I then proceeded to run through a list of things that he'd done. Things we'd never talked about and things we pretended were okay. I gave specific details like when it happened, where we were, and what he did. I told him that I wasn't going to let these moments define me. I've created a new and authentic identity that dismantled the old one that was created for me.

I was surprised at how he quietly listened to a majority of my declaration, but eventually, he couldn't help himself. As I spoke about my authenticity, he cut me off to say that it was "good for me." That my newfound transparency should help me see how full of shit I'd been.

I couldn't say he was wrong.

For years, I lied, pretending to be okay with the abuse. Pretending not to notice how he was abusing those around me. How he subtly took away my freedom at 16 years old. I lied about how I wanted to vomit every time he gave me **that** look. Perhaps I confused him by the way I would go out of my way to get hugs and kisses. In truth, I needed that type of affection from everyone in my life, not just him, but my siblings, my mom, my aunt, and everyone I ever loved.

As I listened to him call me a liar on the phone, I smiled. I couldn't help but find it comical when he said, "I own my shit." Meaning anytime he does something wrong, he owns up to it.

He called me a liar, but for the first time in my life, on that phone call, not a single lie passed through my lips.

A liar? No. Not anymore. But a force of opposition to him? Absolutely.

With my phone between my ear and shoulder, I glided from my master bedroom to my office on auto-pilot, all the while listening to his rebuttal:

"Your marriage is a sham." "You're full of shit." "You're a coward."

Just as I began to zone out from his onslaught of accusations in an attempt to make me the villain, he said something that snatched me from the brink of my daydream back to the clear sound of his voice,

"And all that shit you said happened and what I did... I'm pretty sure you're fabricating it."

My eyes widened. Out of all the madness I'd heard him speak over the years, this one blew me away.

"You're saying I'm making it all up?"

Why did I ask? I knew damn well that's what he was saying.

"Maybe that's what you think happened, but…" I don't know how he finished that sentence because I was audibly laughing.

'What a wild approach to take to this convo,' I thought to myself.

According to him, everything I recounted, I pulled out of thin air. Everything except one event in particular.

A while back, he and I had a discussion about me going to school to pursue my passion for teaching. I had a bit of experience as an English tutor and I absolutely fell in love with it. I expressed this to him and he responded by "warning" me that I would be terrible at it and shouldn't waste my time. His proof was the fact that my younger siblings, whom I would assist with their homework from time to time, weren't faring well in school.

On the phone, he insisted that the conversation never went that way and emphatically stated that I had complete freedom to do whatever I wanted.

"You, out of everyone, could do whatever they wanted," he claimed.

I laughed again. Had he heard himself? That statement proved that he was well aware of the fact that his home was a prison and no one had the freedom to leave or move about, supposedly, except me.

I responded by saying there was no use in us going back and forth. I knew the truth and he would never admit that he, too, was aware of the truth. We ended the conversation by agreeing not to be in each other's lives.

"I know you'll be successful. Have a good life, baby."

Oh, did he know how to play the game! He ended that mess of a call with a warm compliment and a term of endearment so I would wonder if I had indeed been the bad guy.

THE TRANSFORMATION

My husband stayed in the other room to give me privacy during the conversation. The moment I hung up, I ran to him, tears pouring down my face. I buried my face in his shoulder and he squeezed me tight, not saying a word.

After my tears ran dry, I looked up at him with a smile.

I realized that I had just climbed Mount Everest.

I gave him a play-by-play of the whole conversation. When I was complete, he held my face in his hands, kissed me on the lips, and said, "I'm proud of you. I know that wasn't easy."

Damn right, it wasn't easy but as I took a step back from my husband's embrace, I let out a heavy exhale. I'd done it. I faced my fear and conquered it. Nothing else would ever be able to hold me back.

THE IMPACT

Not too long after, I was invited to be spotlighted as a guest on a talk show where we spoke about overcoming and owning trauma. As the discussion continued, I eventually shared my story about the phone call and my climb up Mount Everest. It was an exhilarating experience to be able to share so openly!

After the show, a woman reached out to me and explained that she was in the audience and was moved by my story. She told me that she, too, was haunted by her past abuse. She escaped her abuser, but ever since then, flashes of memories would torment her and cause her to have panic attacks. She informed me that my story gave her the strength to commit to confronting her abuser and finally find her peace.

It was that message that made me realize that I had a much bigger calling. My stories weren't about me at all; not anymore! They're about who I share them with. I dove further into that theory and explored the effect my story had on my business as a book coach. I discovered that my journey was the missing part of the formula that would help me impact the lives of people around the globe.

Using that newly completed formula, I created the framework that I use in my business, in my presentations, and even in this book. Your story and your journey MUST be a part of your formula. It is the vehicle that will deliver transformation and impact to your audience and it's the syrup that makes your book "sticky" so that it sticks with the reader forever.

I must warn you, however. Beware the desire to share for the sake of sharing.

Our stories are powerful but the relationship you have with your audience must be a selfless one. You could go on and on about your journey, the things you've been through, the things that shaped who you are, but if it doesn't resonate with your audience, they won't care.

You are sharing your story because you want to help, inspire, or educate your readers. To ensure your story delivers on this intention, ask yourself, "Why am I telling this story? Is this really what the audience needs to hear from me? Or am I telling it because *I* think it has a powerful message?"

Takeaway: Your story is your greatest asset. Use it to create a deep connection with your audience that gives them the opportunity to see themselves in a new light. Be sure to share that story powerfully and authentically.

CHAPTER 5

Sharing Your Wisdom

In the previous chapter, I stated that your story is merely a part of the formula for impact and transformation. The other part of the formula is the wisdom of the author. You are, after all, the expert and we are looking to you to provide the solution to our biggest challenges.

As businesspeople, we have a lifetime of wisdom that we share with our customers and clients. They rely on us to teach them what they don't know and what they didn't know they didn't know. Some of us do this through the use of workshops, masterminds, one-on-one sessions, and more. These teaching methods are essential to our business structures. However, books have a power that our online offerings do not; the power of forever.

The internet is always upgrading. New programs, new software, new platforms, and, thanks to Web3, a whole new internet. The way we relay information digitally will always change, thus our audience's access to our materials will always be limited.

Books will never have this issue because they are timeless. Even if the format changes (print, audiobook, e-book), your book never disappears. They last for generations as families continue to pass down stories from one generation to the next. This gives you the ability to impact lives even after you die.

Beyond being a major piece of your legacy, a book containing your wisdom is the perfect form of reference for your followers. I'll give you an example.

One of the most impactful courses I ever enrolled in was an online course to help me sharpen my skills as a speaker. Each session contained an average of 10 video lessons, about 25 minutes each. Even though it seemed like a lot of content and information to consume, I moved through it rather quickly. The videos were highly engaging and interactive so I had no problem receiving the information. After completing about half of the course, I took a three-week break. During that time, I was asked to appear as a guest on a popular podcast.

I'd been leveling up as a speaker and I was confident in the topic I was asked to speak on, so

I felt totally prepared. My team created awesome graphics, I posted on my socials about it. I was ready to go! Less than 24 hours before we were meant to go live, I was asked what I wanted the title of the interview to be.

I could have come up with anything! But thanks to my training, I knew better. Early on in the course, we learned about the power of topics and titles, so I knew I had to get this right or else I'd blow my chance at leveraging the video later on.

I had no choice but to log back into the course and get a refresher. Unfortunately, that particular segment didn't have its own session or designated video. I found myself fast-forwarding through multiple 25-minute videos. I searched and I skimmed for what seemed like forever. Eventually, I found the segment I was looking for and was able to come up with a great title.

In that moment, however, I wished there was a written form of that course. If there had been, I would have been able to easily Search and Find the section and even bookmark it for future reference. With a book containing your knowledge, readers would be able to easily refer back to your information forever.

But how much of your knowledge goes into your book? The answer to this question lies in your intention.

Why are you writing this book? Who are you helping and what do you want them to walk away with? Any information you give should be directly related to helping them achieve the results your solution promises. If it doesn't lead to them getting their results, leave it out.

Let's pretend for a moment that I ignore that rule of thumb.

As we both know, my intention for this book is to help you use your own book to take your career to new heights. As an independent publishing expert, I have everything you need to write, produce, publish, and market your book. But two of these have no bearing on the elevation of your career: producing and publishing. While you will need to understand those processes eventually, it would be a waste of time for me to coach you on them now. Instead, I can focus on the fundamentals that you need to get the results you're looking for; writing and marketing.

Everyone wins.

Takeaway: Your wisdom has the potential to last for generations when published in a book. It gives people tangible information that they can refer back to for decades to come. Ensure the information you share is relevant to the value you're promising to give your readers.

CHAPTER 6

Story + Wisdom = IMPACT

Some books contain only the author's wisdom, much like a textbook, and others contain only the author's story and experience, like a memoir. We've all read books like these, but do they offer you transformation? Do they follow you through life? Are they the types of books whose pages, lines, and chapters pop into your head at seemingly random moments?

That's the danger of separating your story from your wisdom; you soften the impact.

Let's take James Baldwin, for example. Many of his non-fiction books are compilations of essays (or an entire essay in and of itself like *The Devil Finds Work*). Now, we know essays are often written for educational purposes and usually stick to delivering information only. But what makes James Baldwin such an impactful author is that his essays perfectly blend wisdom and story to create transformation in the mind and lives of his readers.

The Fire Next Time is the greatest example of this. It's a blend of two essays, "My Dungeon Shook: Letter to my Nephew on the One Hundredth Anniversary of the Emancipation" and "Down at the Cross: Letter from a Region of My Mind."

Both essays teach the reader about the power of fear and how fear serves as the foundation for racism, toxic relationships, and religious beliefs and traditions. This overall message is very clear, yet it is delivered through the use of storytelling.

Baldwin recounts specific moments in his life where fear was the motivating factor for various traumatic moments he experienced. He goes on to break down those moments intellectually and practically to drive the point and help it apply to the reader.

It's like a one-two punch of impact!

The Year of Magical Thinking by Joan Didion is another perfect example. In it, Joan takes the reader through her experience with grief and mourning during the year after her husband's death.

With a story like that, *The Year of Magical Thinking* could have just been a memoir in which Joan merely recounts what happened. Perhaps we would be entertained as readers, but it's not enough, and Joan knew it.

Instead, she incorporated her personal analysis of her grief and backed it up with psychological and medical research and explanations. This helps the reader to be able to understand their own mourning and use this book as a way to overcome their grief. It's not just about Joan; it's also about you, the reader.

The addition of knowledge and information gives her book an entirely new element and is what ultimately led to her book becoming a Pulitzer Prize winner and is used as the "go-to" book to help people deal with grief.

One thing that both Baldwin and Didion did was refrain from thinking about themselves. Despite the fact that their books have large portions of their story incorporated into them, they still kept the reader in mind. They didn't tell their story for the sake of telling their story. Every recount had a purpose and intention, and the intention is written as the solution to a problem the reader is having.

For Baldwin, the intention was to help Americans understand how fear dictates action and how that fear keeps them from seeing the struggle of Black Americans.

Keeping that at the front of his mind, every sentence was written to fulfill that intention. Every story was a brick laid in the road to reach that purpose and ultimately change the mindset of the reader.

For Didion, the problem was that the reader is going through a grieving period and they don't know how to find their way out of mourning. Her intention is to help them out of their grief and she does this by using her own experiences, knowledge, and medical facts.

So, ask yourself, "What is my intention? What is the purpose of my book, and what are readers supposed to get out of it?"

Answer these questions and use them to determine what goes into your book and what stories you will share to back up any solutions you offer.

Takeaway: In order to generate impact for your readers, you must combine your story and your wisdom into the structure of your book. Remember that the book is not about you, it's about them. What will they get out of it and how can your story and knowledge give them that? Be intentional about what you share.

PART

III

USING THE BOOK

Using Your Book to Strengthen Your Credibility

No matter the type of book you publish, the topic you write about, or the genre it is in, publishing a book will always make people look at you differently. Some call it showcasing your expertise, others call it boosting your credibility. Regardless of how you describe this outcome, publishing a book instantly changes your status.

We often use the idiom, "He wrote the book on it."

We don't usually mean this literally. We're simply attempting to express the fact that an individual is a verified expert on a given topic. But have you ever thought about where that expression came from? Has it ever occurred to you that this phrase is living proof of the power of a book, not just for the reader but also for the author?

As an author, you are expected to be the vessel of knowledge, the source of wisdom, and the oracle that has the answers and solutions to your reader's problems. When you satisfy that expectation, your credibility is strengthened, and you firmly position yourself as the expert in the eyes of your reader.

We're all coming to you because you literally wrote the book on it.

Let us not forget, however, that in order to obtain the status of a true expert, you must be a powerful author. Every word on every page must be saturated with the kept promise. Your integrity must be overflowing. Your intention must be crystal clear. You must remain selfless as you pour value into every sentence. If you can accomplish this, your credibility will never be questioned.

Your book isn't just a display of your wisdom, it's also an opportunity for your followers. In this modern age of social media, we all have followers, some more than others, but we all have a group of individuals who desire to be educated, be inspired, or be motivated by us.

Many of these people will never get a chance to actually know you, they'll never be able to speak to you, and they'll never get the full effect of what you have to offer. Yearn as they might, they may never have the chance to work with you or study under you. Yet, they need you. Their problems are becoming more than burdensome, they're hopeless. They've been following you, and up till now, they've only gotten bits and pieces of your solution. It's not enough.

The release of your book gives your followers the ability to become mentees from a distance. Finally, they get the answers they've been seeking. Your book will serve as the textbook they never knew they needed, the manual to solving their problems. These followers become your students. Their lives will be forever changed because of what you wrote.

This is what will lead to real, well-crafted, heartfelt book reviews.

Whenever we, as consumers, get our hands on something that blows our minds or changes our lives, all we want to do is share it. Share it with our followers, with our family and friends, and with the entire Internet. Without being asked or incentivized, we begin to write reviews. We want others to know about the beautiful transformation we've experienced.

Without even trying, you'll find that you have honest reviews from people you've never met. Those reviews will lead to more eyes on your book which leads to more purchases, and that leads to more impacted lives. Soon, everyone understands that you are the expert.

But what good is having that credibility if we can't leverage it?

I have found that most business owners desire to be paid to speak. Many of us seek these opportunities. We've done the guest appearances, the free workshops, masterclasses, and summits, but we crave for much more. The bigger stages. The ones where the event organizers are willing to pay for the speakers.

Having gained true credibility from your book, you would be in a prime position to be paid to step onto those stages.

There are many things I've learned from my speaking coach, but one thing she made sure I understood is the simple fact that corporate event organizers are never searching for speakers. They're searching for experts. They are looking for people who have the expertise to come and share it with their audiences. Having a published book (or multiple books) is the social proof they're looking for. Having powerful reviews from a number of people for that book further validates that proof.

Your book and the credibility that comes with it serve as the springboard to the major speaking engagements.

Action Steps:

1. **Get Featured as an Author on a Podcast**

    Podcast hosts love featuring authors because they're usually a wealth of knowledge and can offer real value to listeners. Not only will this increase your visibility and your online presence, but it'll also increase the number of people who see you as the expert.

2. **Reposition Yourself on Social Media**

    If your social media profile does not help you show up as an expert, you should consider revamping it. When we Google you, we should be able to clearly see what you do and what you're an expert on. Your socials (like

Facebook, Instagram, Twitter, and LinkedIn) should reflect what you want to be remembered for.

3. Begin Publishing Articles

Whether you do guest posting or you simply publish articles to your LinkedIn profile, this is another great way to solidify your credibility. It works the same way a book does but in a much more condensed version. Readers will be able to read your wisdom and your story and be impacted by it.

CHAPTER 8

Using Your Book to Establish Your Thought Leadership

Thought leadership can be defined in several different ways. For me, I've always defined a thought leader as "someone who has an innovative way of thinking, doing, or being, and they share that way with their audience and cause true transformation in the lives of their followers."

I would also say that a thought leader can be seen as a "disruptor." A disruptor is an individual or organization that disrupts the status quo of a current system, regime, or process, usually by introducing a new and innovative way of thinking, doing, or being. The very concept of disruption is what makes thought leaders truly powerful individuals. They have the ability to see the unseen and to understand the misunderstood.

Ava DuVernay. Simon Sinek. Greta Thunberg. For decades, these three global disruptors have been successfully expanding their thought leadership by changing the way we tell stories, the way we improve leadership, and the way we understand global climate change. Their innovation is actively shaping the world today.

You are no different.

Throughout the growth of your business, you have tapped into and cultivated your innovation. Perhaps you've had the opportunity to share with others and gotten a taste of the impact you can create. But what would it look like for you if you were able to share your innovation with tens of thousands of people? What would it look like for you if you were considered a true thought leader?

Revel in that for a moment.

Imagine that someone is introducing you. They say your name, your title, your area of expertise, and then they say "Thought Leader."

Say it aloud. Listen to what it sounds like.

Being called a thought leader adds an entirely new dimension to people's perceptions of you. You aren't just an expert on a particular topic, you are THE expert. You are the one who not only has deep knowledge of the subject but has also gone beyond that knowledge and created a completely new concept within it.

From developing powerful connections to building your brand and reputation and even motivating your team members, being considered a thought leader opens the door to opportunities and possibilities previously thought to be closed.

It's important to remember that if you don't share that innovation, you're not a thought leader; you're just another expert.

A book that shares your innovation and expertise, however, will be your audience's introduction to your thought leadership. Your innovation and knowledge, along with your story, will be woven into the pages of your book, giving your audience the opportunity to be impacted by your influence.

Let's take Brené Brown, for example.

Before the release of her book "The Gift of Imperfection," Brown was relatively unknown. Working as a social worker and research professor, she poured her wisdom, her story, and her research into various publications and articles, including a blog on her website. In 2010, with the help of Hazelden Publishing, she released her book to the public. This book went on to become a bestseller and ultimately cemented her position as a thought leader and drastically spread her influence across the globe. With the release of her second and third books, Brown's thought leadership was firmly in place, and she became known as one of the leading experts on vulnerability.

What will your thought leadership look like? Where will it take you? Will you be on the TED stage? Will you get the free feature in Forbes Magazine? Understand that wherever your thought leadership takes you, it is your book that will get you there.

Action Steps:

1. **Apply for TED or TEDx**

   Besides a book, TED and TEDx are arguably one of the best platforms to use to expand your thought leadership. This global stage has seen the likes of Amy Cuddy, Elon Musk, Chimamanda Ngozi Adichie, Steve Jobs, Stacey Abrams, and many more.

   As a TEDx speaker myself, I can attest to the power this platform has. Being able to share my innovation on this global stage has changed the way people see and interact with me, which has aided in the expansion of my business and the up-leveling of my career.

2. Start a Podcast

Having a podcast can give you the opportunity to continually share your wisdom with a large audience. You have free reign to discuss whatever topics are important to you and touch the lives of your listeners. If you can come up with enough valuable content to keep your audience engaged, then you will be able to spread your thought leadership consistently for years to come.

CHAPTER 9

Using Your Book at Events

As business owners, we all understand the importance of networking. Many businesses would fail if not for the power of networking. That's why there are thousands of networking events that take place across the entire globe every year. Summits, conferences, trade shows, meetups, workshops, seminars, the list is endless.

We find ourselves attending these events in the hopes of rubbing elbows with potential business partners or investors. Yet, the typical outcome is that we simply learn information and go back to our businesses and attempt to apply it. The biggest issue is that we spend money to attend and then fail to immediately make that money back, let alone profit. There is, however, a way to get much more out of these events, and it's all based on the way you position yourself.

Being an author and having your book available at an event allows you to earn, what I call, the 3 C's: **connections**, **credibility,** and **cash**. You don't have to attend these events simply hoping to get value from them; the pursuit of these 3 C's guarantees both immediate and future success.

There are three surefire ways to earn the 3 C's with your book at almost any networking event. Keep in mind, however, that each event is different. The rules and procedures surrounding selling products or marketing will vary. It is your responsibility to ensure that you are in line with the rules set forth by event organizers.

1. Get a Table and Become a Vendor

Most networking events offer spaces for vendors to sell their products to attendees throughout the day. These vendors arrange tables and exhibit spaces to showcase their products or services and attract customers to come and buy or learn more.

You can use this opportunity to showcase and sell your book. With a beautifully arranged table, testimonials, and marketing materials, you can sell copies of your book to your potential readers and have live conversations with them about what they're going to get from it. These conversations will make both you and your book memorable.

To become a vendor, many organizers have a list of qualifications, requirements, and fees. So, before you apply, make sure that the types of people who are attending the event are your ideal readers. They must be within your target audience for you to resonate with them and eventually invite them to buy. If the people the event is targeting don't align with the general audience for your book, then don't waste your time and money attempting to become a vendor.

2. Become a Sponsor

If you want to go above and beyond, become a sponsor. Sponsors assist event organizers with funds and other resources to make the event successful. It is common practice for organizers to offer their sponsors perks like speaking opportunities, a booth/exhibit, exclusive networking opportunities, and more. With these perks, you will be given the opportunity to inform people about (and sell) your book, all while describing your business and what you offer. Your book will help back up any claims you make regarding your expertise.

Becoming a sponsor may require a sizeable investment but can garner a significant return. However, similar to being a vendor, you must ensure that this audience is the right audience for you. It could be devastating to become a sponsor only to have the attendees care less about what you do or what you offer. Weigh all of your options carefully before making this decision.

3. Distribute Marketing Materials

If being a vendor or becoming a sponsor is not feasible, you can still make waves with your book. Having marketing materials at a networking event is absolutely essential. Oftentimes, simply handing out basic business cards with your information doesn't cut it. People rarely go through the work of saving your name and number in their phones. Your approach must be much more targeted than this.

At the event, you are going to tell a number of people about your book and many of them will say that they are interested in it. The game is to get these people to buy your book on the spot.

In my experience, the best, non-invasive way to do this is through the use of a QR Code. A QR code (or Quick-Response code) is a black-and-white grid that is scanned with a smartphone camera or app and takes the user to a pre-determined website. You can create a QR Code that takes users to your website, bookstore, landing page, or wherever your book is available for purchase, and in just a few clicks, they can buy it.

This code can be printed on almost any material: business cards, flyers, banners, t-shirts, and more. Given that you're attending a networking event, a business card may be more appropriate. Have the code printed on a card and offer it to the person you're speaking with. Invite them to scan the card right then and there and share more deeply about the book and what they'll get out of it.

Using one of these three strategies, you'll be able to use your book to help you earn credibility, connections, and cash at every event you attend.

Action Steps:

1. Practice Your Pitch

It's essential to be as clear and succinct as possible when describing your book. The goal isn't to tell them everything they'll get out of it. You want to tell them just enough to understand the concept and desire to know more. Try explaining what your book is about in 20 words or less, then memorize it. Whenever someone asks you what your book is about, this is what you will say.

If you need help with articulation, you can look at the New York Times bestsellers list. With every book listed, there is a small blurb that offers insight into what the book is about. Notice how they are short, sweet, and to the point, all while enticing you to want to know more. Try to follow the same style for your pitch.

2. Prepare Marketing Material

Whether it's the QR code business cards or flyers, be sure to give the people you meet something to remember you by.

3. **Prepare a Follow-Up Sequence Before the Event**

   Before the event, write up an email sequence for those you will meet. You will email them after the event, thanking them for the connection and potentially reminding them to go and buy the book.

4. **Bring Your Books**

   Whether you're a vendor, a sponsor, or just an attendee, make sure you come to the event with several copies of your book (or QR codes if your book is digital). You never know who you'll encounter and who will want to buy from you.

5. **Collect Business Cards of Those Interested**

   While others may trash business cards they've been given, you will collect and keep them. Collect a business card from anyone who said they were interested in your book and ask them for permission to email them regarding more information about the book. This will help you grow your email list and give you a leg up when you begin an email marketing campaign for your book.

CHAPTER 10

Monetizing Your Book

Many people are under the impression that in order to make money off of your book, you must sell tens of thousands of copies. While that would be a nice feat, it is quite difficult to achieve. The truth is, every book has over a dozen streams of revenue. The more creative you are, the higher number of revenue streams you can reach. With these various income streams, you can quickly get a return on your investment and make a generous and continuous profit.

The key to book monetization is understanding that your book is not just a product, it's a business. You can either run it as a standalone business or integrate it with your existing one. Either way, in order to be successful, you must become an authorpreneur. As an authorpreneur, you will use business strategies and techniques to manage, produce, and promote your book. Never forget that this isn't about selling, it's about building.

Just like with any business, you must establish a brand for your book. What are its values? What does it represent? How would you describe the look and feel of it? Who does it serve? What is its purpose?

When you have the brand and target audience in place, you will have a clear picture of what and how to offer it to them. Once you know that, you can then focus on marketing strategies and how to take your book to the next level.

Before we dive into the ways to monetize your book, we must first look at the number one way to maximize your profit.

There has been a long-standing belief that in order to be successful as an author, you must publish your book through a traditional publishing house. This would include the likes of Penguin Random House, HarperCollins, and Simon & Schuster. Scoring a deal with any of these major houses would be a dream come true for many people, but there are several roadblocks that could challenge that aspiration.

Firstly, for many, it takes years to be recognized by a medium or large traditional publishing house. This is because they receive thousands of submissions a year. Unless you are a celebrity or influencer, the likelihood of being quickly recognized by any of the major publishers is incredibly low.

Secondly, there have been proven cases of gender and racial discrimination by a number of publishing houses over the years. Being a woman and/or a person of color serves as a "disadvantage," as some houses believe it goes against what their audience desires and hurts their bottom line. Thus, you are likely to be overlooked.

Lastly, with traditional publishing, you do not own the rights to your book. This is an issue for many reasons. To begin, this means that you do not get 100% revenue on the sales of your book.

On average, an author receives about 8 to 15% royalty, and most times, authors are expected to do quite a bit of marketing on their own. You also do not get creative control. Any title that you may have chosen or even the vision for the book cover design may be changed based on the discretion of the house.

The biggest issue is that you cannot control the trajectory of your book or career. If you wish to leverage your book in a specific way, perhaps in your business, you may be prohibited from doing so. If you wish to re-release your book, add a new edition, or turn it into a series, your publishing house may prohibit it if it doesn't align with their desired outcome.

Between the time it takes, the discrimination, and the loss of rights, many authors choose to follow the independent publishing route. With independent publishing (AKA self-publishing), you are free to do the market research yourself, select your target audience, and design the book the way you want to. You maintain 100% of your revenue and can leverage your book in any way you choose.

As an authorpreneur and business owner, independent publishing is the best way to maximize the success of your book and its earning potential.

That being said, if your book has become a success after independently publishing it, you've sold a high number of copies, and made a substantial profit, you and your book may catch the attention of a traditional publishing house.

If this is the case, they are likely to make a sweet offer to buy the rights to your book. If and when this happens, my suggestion would be to take it. You would have effectively bypassed issues one and two, and the third issue will be a lot easier to accept with a higher royalty rate and a beautiful publishing deal for future books.

This is what Robert Kiyosaki did. He self-published "Rich Dad Poor Dad" in 1997. Simply through word-of-mouth, thanks to the value and impact his book had, it became a bestseller. This caught the attention of Warner Business Books. Making a deal with Kiyosaki, in 2000, they released a revised edition of the already-famous book and went on to sell millions of copies worldwide.

This path is far easier to traverse than having a literary agent plead with a traditional publisher to look at your manuscript.

Now that you know the best way to maximize your profit, let's take a look at the top five ways to monetize your book.

1. Sell As Is

Selling the book as is will be the main way to earn money from it. Whether it's available for purchase on Amazon, Barnes & Noble, or on your website, your book needs to be readily available for purchase at all times. Anyone who comes across you, your website, or your social media profiles should be instantly made aware of your book and directed to purchase it.

2. Release an Audiobook

Audiobooks are a great way to expand your readership. The ease and convenience of audiobooks cannot and should not be overlooked. According to Grand View Research[1], the audiobook industry was valued at $5,364.9 million in 2022 and is expected to increase by 26.3% from 2023 to 2030. Failing

---

[1] Grand View Research. (2021). Audiobooks Market Size, Share & Trends Analysis Report By Genre (Fiction, Non-Fiction), By Application (Education, Entertainment), By Device (Smartphones, Laptops), By Regions, And Segment Forecasts, 2021-2028. https://www.grandviewresearch.com/industry-analysis/audiobooks-market

to tap into this industry would be a grave mistake. With platforms like ACX, you can easily hire a professional voice-over actor and release your book on Audible, arguably the most popular audiobook platform in the world.

3. Create a Masterclass or Workshop

Most impactful books give readers the ability to learn something truly valuable. Bits and pieces of the information you include in your book can be used to create a short masterclass or workshop. You can charge a small fee for attendees to join. At the end of the session, you can offer a discount on the price of your book and encourage them to buy in order to further their knowledge or gain deeper clarity.

Try to do one masterclass or workshop each month to continue bringing in new potential readers regularly.

4. Create an Online Course

Turning your book into an online course is a great way to offer truly valuable knowledge and transformation to your audience while making a great profit. This online course breaks down the content of your book into a more easily digestible format. You may choose to go deeper into the concepts and ideals your book teaches to add more value and help your readers achieve an even greater understanding. You may even encourage your students to purchase your book to assist them as they journey through the program.

5. Make It a Part of Your Business Funnel (Downsell/Upsell)

As a business owner, you can offer your book to your existing customer base by including it in your funnel. Consider having your book available as a downsell for those who are unable to work with you directly. Whether the issue is time, money, or commitment, your book can serve as a great option for those who want to be in your world without investing too much. Your book can also be an upsell for any freebies you offer. If you give away free information (speaking engagements, any free digital downloads, or free masterclasses), you can encourage your audience to take the next step or increase their chances of success/transformation by buying your book.

With these top five monetization tips, not only will you sell more books and earn more money, but you also expand the reach of your book and get it in front of more eyes that matter.

PART

IV

ABOVE AND BEYOND
FOR YOUR BOOK
(BONUS CHAPTER)

CHAPTER 11

How to Write Your Book

In the original outline of this book, "How to Write Your Book" was not included as a chapter. I intended to completely avoid this topic. The fact of the matter is, how you write your book is of little importance if you don't know how to birth the author within, conceptualize and birth the book idea, and understand how to leverage it. The above must be fully and deeply understood and finalized before you put pen to paper.

However, I found myself asking, "Would this book be truly valuable if I didn't explain how to write one?" I would argue yes, but I would still have a bit of back and forth in my mind about it. So, I resolved to move forward.

My only request is that before you read this chapter, you go back through the previous chapters and resolve the following (Be sure to write your responses down):

1. Who are you? What is your worth? What do you want to be remembered for?

2. What is the promise you wish to deliver to your readers?
3. Are you a person of integrity? How do you plan to practice integrity?
4. What will your legacy be?
5. What is the story you wish to tell?
6. What is the knowledge you wish to share?
7. How do you plan to combine the two?
8. What do you hope this book will do for you or your career?
9. How do you intend to make that happen?
10. What practical steps will you take to achieve this goal?

Assuming you have resolved everything, you can begin to write powerfully and intentionally.

Many people find book writing daunting. The idea of having to come up with tens of thousands of words to put on paper in the correct order and ensure they make sense can seem overwhelming. This is usually due to a lack of preparation that takes place before writing begins. In your case, you will complete all of the prep work necessary, which will leave you excited and ready to power through the writing process and avoid the overwhelm.

Things To Do Before You Begin Writing

1. **Understand Your Audience**
2. **Get Clear on Their Pains and Problems**
3. **Plan Out Your Solutions**
4. **Word Vomit**
5. **Create an Outline Template**
6. **Fill In Outline**

Understand Your Audience

Throughout this journey, you have learned that the most impactful books are written with intention and serve a purpose for the reader. You got clear on the simple fact that readers are selfish and it is your job to give them what they desire. But how can you do this if you don't know who your audience is?

As a business owner, you may already have an established audience, but if your book doesn't speak directly to that audience's desires, you will fail to deliver what they want. This may mean reaching out to people you believe your book would be perfect for and picking their brains to understand what they want and need. Pitch your book idea to them and see how it resonates. Is it missing anything? Is there something that should be addressed?

Don't be afraid to tweak or completely change your idea. I understand that it can be difficult to let go of an idea that you've held on to for years, but if you find that this idea does not resonate with your audience, you must be willing to adjust.

Get Clear on Their Pains and Problems

One commonality between the most impactful books ever written is that they serve as the solution to a problem readers have. Whether it's something as simple as boredom or something more complex like financial instability, the best books always solve a problem.

You have to have a clear understanding of the true pains your readers have. What keeps them up at night? What brings about anxiety and frustration for them? What is it that they want but don't have?

When you know what's hurting, you can potentially fix it.

The mistake many authors make is failing to look into the pains of their audience before attempting to force-feed a solution. Don't be that type of author. Be selfless in your intention to help your readers by actually finding out what they're struggling with.

Plan Out Your Solutions

Even if you already had a solution in mind, rethink it to make sure this solution helps your audience fix their problems. For many of us, the solution may be used in our businesses as a framework or methodology, a step-by-step process, or an easy-to-follow formula. While this may serve as a solution for our clients/customers, it may not be exactly what your reader needs.

Tweak your solution so that it solves your readers' problems and gives them added value.

Word Vomit

This is perhaps my favorite writing technique. Word Vomit is when you take a clean sheet of blank paper (printer paper, preferably) and write everything that comes to mind about your book.

There should be no form and no order. Just write all over the page.

The reason book writing can be so difficult is because of the internal dialogue that goes on when we try to conceptualize and write at the same time. You think to yourself, "I should mention this. I should write that. I might want to discuss this. It's important for me to note that." Then you begin to ask, "Well, how do I say this? What's the best way to word that? When do I mention this?" This goes on and on while you write and keeps you from being able to focus.

Word vomit gives you the ability to get it all out of your head. You can write down the concepts you may want to touch on, sentences that you'll want to include, and quotes or references you may want to add. This is the time to write anything and everything, even if it doesn't make sense. Once you've cleared your mind, you can look back on what you've written and determine what stays and what goes.

Keeping your audience's pains and problems in mind along with your Author's Promise, ask yourself what is necessary. What on that page will aid in delivering a solution? Circle or highlight everything you feel is essential.

You may find yourself needing to word vomit several times. I recommend setting aside 15 minutes a day for three to five days. Each day will bring about something different and give you a higher chance of uncovering valuable gems you'll want to include in your book.

Create an Outline Template

Now that you have a general idea of what the book will contain, you can create a vague outline of what you will address and when. This includes the main points/topics and the solution (or solutions) and will serve as a guide when you begin writing.

Here's an example:

1. Introduction
2. Main Point 1 (Reader's First Problem)
3. Main Point 2 (Reader's Second Problem)
4. Solution 1
5. My Story A
6. Solution 2
7. My Story B

8. Added Value 1
9. Added Value 2
10. Closing

An outline template helps me to map out how I am going to present my information to my reader. I already know that I want to include the reader's problem, the solution, my story to back it up, and added value to give them even more. But being able to map it out allows me to ensure these points are addressed in an appropriate order.

Now, this example is very simple and unoriginal, but it doesn't have to be. As the author, you can get creative with the presentation of information. Perhaps you tell your entire story first or you incorporate references, graphics, or images. The choice is yours.

Fill In Outline

With the results of your word vomit in mind, you can fill in the finer details inside of the outline template. Any sentences or ideas you've written down may be perfectly nestled under one of your main points. Or perhaps a reference you wanted to make would fit within Solution 2. Take the time to write this information in your template.

Be sure, however, that your full outline includes the names of "Main Point" or "Solutions." You want to get as specific as possible with as many details as possible. Spend a significant amount of time building out this outline, as this is what you will use to begin writing. If you can map out your book with specific details, when you begin writing, you will only need to focus on "how to say it" and not "what to say."

With the prep work complete, you can now begin writing.

While you don't want to rush the writing process, be sure to set a deadline for when you'd like to be finished to give yourself some accountability. If you are able to set aside 2-3 hours a day, I would recommend attempting to complete one chapter a day. Keep in mind that the original draft doesn't have to be perfect; it just has to be written. Once completed, you can go back to rework, rewrite, and tweak anything that doesn't resonate.

So, pick up your pen and begin birthing your book.

Final Thoughts

When I began writing this book, I was insanely confident in my ability to teach you as a reader. I said to myself, "This is going to be awesome. I'm going to show them how to birth their book and it'll be easy."

I should have known better. I have helped dozens of authors birth their books and I would have never used the word "easy" to describe the process.

What was I thinking?

But that's the thing about deciding to write a book. You think you know everything about a particular topic so you feel confident enough to write about it. Perhaps you did. Perhaps you truly are the #1 authority in your niche, but it doesn't change the fact that you will learn even more as you write.

This concept was mind-blowing to me.

This book teaches you the exact same framework I use in my business. In writing the book, I wanted to show examples from known authors to have used a variation of it. But when I found that almost every globally influential author used the exact methodology that I *thought* I created, I was flabbergasted.

I went down a 3-week rabbit hole of reading and researching the different ways my framework was being used throughout literary history. The more I read, the more I learned about what makes a great non-fiction book powerful. I was able to tweak my framework to include key characteristics and further increase the possibility for deep impact on readers.

I've poured what I learned onto these pages and my hope is that your life is forever changed by it. I pray that my methodologies serve you in a way that leaves you enriched, empowered, and excited to birth your book the right way.

Your journey to becoming a world-renowned author is unlikely to be a simple one but it's not impossible. With the right help, you can birth your book and leverage it in a way that works for you and your career, and that is what I am here to do.

Scan the QR code below to see how we can work together.

About the Author

Porsché Mysticque Steele is a professional speaker, independent book publishing expert, and CEO of MysticqueRose Publishing Services.

As a TEDx speaker, book coach, and one of the youngest black female self-publishing experts, she helps high-performing CEOs combine their story and wisdom to publish highly impactful books that generate income, influence, and expands their thought leadership.

Keeping her core values of communication, integrity, and supporting others at the forefront of everything she does, Porsché and her team continue to unlock the stories and knowledge that business owners have and help them share it powerfully in books that bring about true impact for their readers.

When she's not birthing books, she assists organizations with improving their team's productivity and company branding through the use of storytelling. As a powerful keynote speaker, she also helps college students with establishing their identity to find the strength to pursue their purpose, dreams, and careers without feeling unsure or unstable.

Porsché Mysticque is originally from Pittsburgh, Pennsylvania, but currently resides in Nigeria with her husband.

Scan the QR code to connect with Porsché Mysticque Steele.